D1442615

Sleepover Party

WITHDRAWN

DK | Penguin Random House

Senior Designer Wendy Bartlet
Project Editor Laura Palosuo
Designers Eleanor Bates, Charlotte Bull, Rachael Hare
Assistant Editor Sophia Danielsson-Waters
US Senior Editor Shannon Beatty
US Editor Margaret Parrish
Photographer Dave King
Illustrator Rachael Hare
Jacket Designer Wendy Bartlet
Pre-production Andy Hilliard, Dragana Puvacic
Producer Georgina Russell
Creative Technical Support Sonia Charbonnier
Managing Editor Penny Smith
Managing Art Editor Gemma Glover
Art Director Jane Bull
Publisher Mary Ling

First American Edition, 2016
Published in the United States by DK Publishing
345 Hudson Street, New York, New York 10014

Copyright © 2016 DK, a Division of Penguin Random House LLC
16 17 18 19 20 10 9 8 7 6 5 4 3 2 1
001–285434–February/2016

All rights reserved.
Without limiting the rights under the copyright reserved above, no part of this publication
may be reproduced, stored in or introduced into a retrieval system, or transmitted, in any
form, or by any means (electronic, mechanical, photocopying, recording, or otherwise),
without the prior written permission of the copyright owner.
Published in Great Britain by Dorling Kindersley Limited.

A catalog record for this book is available from the Library of Congress.
ISBN: 978-1-4654-5097-5
DK books are available at special discounts when purchased
in bulk for sales promotions, premiums, fund-raising, or educational use.
For details, contact: DK Publishing Special Markets, 345 Hudson Street,
New York, New York 10014 or
SpecialSales@dk.com

Printed and bound in China by RR Donnelley

All images © Dorling Kindersley Limited
For further information see: www.dkimages.com

A WORLD OF IDEAS
SEE ALL THERE IS TO KNOW

www.dk.com

SAFETY

This book is packed with things to do—some are simple, while others are more tricky. We hope you enjoy this book, but please be sensible and safe. **Tell an adult before you do any of the projects, carefully read all the instructions, and seek help whenever you need it,** especially for **cooking, cutting, and sewing.** Whenever you see:

please ask an adult for help. The publisher cannot take responsibility for the outcome, injury, loss, damage, or mess that occurs as a result of you attempting any of the activities in this book.

Contents

Party planner

All the best parties need prep work. Think about what you want, talk to an adult, and make a list. Use the notes on this page to help you plan.

Invitations

To make your guests feel extra special, you may want to send invitations by mail. Include the date, time, address, and what each guest needs to bring. A map or directions are also helpful.

Party Ideas

Will your party have a theme? We have some great ideas and inspiration (pages 6-15). Will you choose a marvelous movie night or a super spa bash?

Food and Drinks

Start by checking if there are any foods your guests can't eat. Talk to an adult to sort out ideas for the main meal and breakfast. Other things to think about are drinks, snacks, and perhaps a midnight feast!

Activities

It's good to have some activities prepared just in case you're stuck for what to do. Luckily, this book has lots of ideas that'll entertain everyone!

Sleeping

Where will your guests sleep? Tell them in advance if they need to bring a sleeping bag, pillow, or blanket. Make a plan before the party starts, so you don't have to figure out arrangements when you're all tired.

Party Bags

Giving out party bags is a great way to thank your guests for coming. Look on pages 74-75 for inspiration on what to put inside.

Party idea:
Pamper party

A luxurious pamper party is a great way to unwind, relax, and treat your friends. Hang up pretty decorations, put on soothing music, and become the best spa in town!

Find out how to make these hanging heart decorations on page 76. You can also use the heart templates for bunting.

A DIY foot spa is super soothing for your soles.

Pamper your nails

No spa party is complete without a manicure. Head to pages 16-17 for nail art inspiration. You can also do pedicures after you've tried the foot spa on pages 22-23.

How to make pom-pom decorations

1 Fold a few sheets of tissue paper back and forth, accordion-style.

2 Cut off the accordion's corners. Tie thread around it.

3 Separate and fluff out the layers on either side.

Hang paper pom-poms for a stylish and sophisticated look.

Fruity facials (pages 18-19) and comfy eye masks (pages 38-39) are pamper party essentials!

Invitations

You can use the eye mask template on page 78 for your spa sleepover invitations.

Use plainer paper on the front and glue patterned paper on the back.

Pamper Party
To:

Time:

Place:

Date:

Use colorful envelopes to complement your invitations.

Party idea: Campout

Bring the outdoors inside with your own crazy, cool camping party. Set up a pretend campfire as the center of the action, tell stories, play games, and giggle the whole night long!

Send invitations that guests can open like a tent!

Put up signs for rooms! Make the bathroom the "outhouse." The kitchen can be the "picnic area."

Prepare a scavenger hunt. Compile a list of things guests need to find. The first person to get them all wins!

For bunting, cut out diamonds from a fabric. Fold them over a ribbon to make triangle shapes. Staple to secure. ⚠

Campout invitations

Copy the template on page 77 onto card stock.

⚠ Cut along this line.

Fold out along the dotted lines.

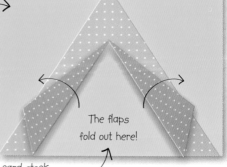

Glue the tent sides onto a piece of colored card stock.

The flaps fold out here!

Write details on the card stock underneath the flaps.

Mini teepees

You may need to ask an adult for help because this craft is a bit tricky. Hold 5 garden stakes together and tie them at the top. Pull the bottom of the stakes out to make a circle. Next, hang a sheet or blanket around the stakes. Tie at the top to secure.

Use clothespins to hold open the front flaps.

Tie the stakes with string.

Sit in a circle and tell spooky stories!

There's no need to make a real fire— this one's made of yellow and red tissue paper, logs, and stones.

Make the dreamcatcher on pages 42-43.

9

Party idea: Fashion

If you love clothes, crafting, and customizing, a super-stylish fashion-themed party will be just up your alley. Get creative with your hair, outfits, and shoes, then you're ready to strut your stuff!

Bling Rings

Make these funky rings (pages 50-51). Choose colors that match your outfits.

Find out how to make these sweet tutus on pages 56-57.

Don't forget to take the quiz on pages 34-35 to find out what type of fashionista you are!

Invitations

For fashionable invitations, copy the handbag template on page 77 onto pretty card stock.

Fashion Sleepover

Write all your party information on the front.

How to make chains

Patterned paper-chain decorations work well for a fancy fashion theme.

⚠️

1

Cut lots of strips of different patterned paper, 1in (3cm) wide and 12in (30cm) long.

2

To make a loop, place two strips on top of each other, patterned sides facing out. Staple the ends together.

3

Keep making loops, securing each one by stapling together through the previous loop. Make the chain as long as you like.

Make these funky, chunky bangles on pages 46-47.

Revamp a pair of flip-flops! For inspiration, head to pages 62-63.

Hair Styling

You can't have a fashion party without hair styling! Learn how to create different styles (pages 20-21) or create your own clip-in hair wraps (pages 60-61).

11

Party idea: Pop star

You don't have to love singing to be a pop star. It's all about the attitude! Put up funky decorations, play some good music, and have a karaoke or jam session!

Hang up blank CDs for glitzy decorations, or use them as coasters.

VIP invitations

Make your invitations look like VIP passes! Write the party details on card stock, make a hole in the top, and add a long ribbon. Give these to your guests to hang around their necks. Only let them in if they show their passes!

VIP ★ pass

Rocking sneakers

Want that ultimate rock star look? Jazz up your favorite plain canvas sneakers (pages 58-59) to add a cool step to your dance routines.

Nibble on perfect pizzas using the recipe on pages 70-71.

For rock-star bunting, use the templates on page 79. Gold, glittery card stock looks amazing.

Keep the music going with lots of tunes everyone

likes. Play some sing-along classics.

You'll look like cool rock stars sipping on yummy mocktails (pages 66-67).

Sip on your mocktails through funky straws. Find decoration templates on page 79.

13

Party idea: Movie night

Making movies the main feature of your party is a totally top idea. They are fantastic to watch—and there are so many fun film activities you can do, plus ways to set the scene. And... action!

Use the frames from pages 26-27 to take movie star photos.

INVITATION

TO ....

DATE ....

Nothing says "the movies" more than invitations styled to look like clapperboards!

For bunting, find some stars and stripes paper, cut out diamonds, and then fold over a long piece of ribbon. Staple to secure in place.

Go to pages 68-69 to find a great way to make popcorn. How can you have a movie night without it?

Candy bangles

Sit and watch movies with candy bangles on your wrists (pages 52-53). Try not to finish them before the movie's over!

Lay out a "red carpet" for your guests at the entrance of your home.

1 Paint two large dots, then add a smaller one underneath.

2 Smooth the sides to create a pretty heart shape.

Simple dots work best when you use contrasting colors.

Pretty heart

Polka dots

2 Use another color to add a dot in the middle of the daisy.

Crazy daisy

1 Make five equal dots in a circle. Let dry.

Nail art

It's so much fun to give someone a manicure! Paint a base coat first and let dry. Then try out these pretty designs. And remember to keep the grown-ups happy—don't spill your polish on your clothes, carpets, or furniture!

1

Before you start, make sure your hands are clean. Paint your first base coat, and let it dry. Apply a few base coats in this way.

Base coat

1 Use a pink base coat, then add black dots.

Sweet strawberry

Lovely ladybug

2 When dry, add a spiked green pattern for the leaves.

1 Paint a black semicircle and a line on a red base. Let dry.

2 Add spots and two white dots for eyes. When dry, add pupils.

16

1 Paint one large circle and two small dots for the ears. Let dry.

2 Paint a semicircle in a lighter color. When dry, add eyes and nose.

Cuddly bear

Vary dots in different sizes for a fun, bold look.

Spots in a row

Stuff you'll need! • Nontoxic, peel-off nail polish
• Toothpicks

Magic stick!

2

Use the toothpick for an easy way to make dots or patterns. Dip it in polish and touch it lightly to the nail.

1 Paint two big white dots for the eyes.

Eye see you!

2 When dry, add black pupils inside the white dots.

Cute bunny

Puppy paw

1 Paint a semicircle on the bottom half of the nail, then add oval ears.

2 When dry, paint on eyes and a nose with a different color.

Try different sized dots for a cute puppy paw print.

17

Fruity facials

It turns out that fruit isn't just yummy in your tummy—it's great for your skin, too! These facials are a little luxury that will make you feel pampered. Keep on for 10-20 minutes, then rinse with warm water.

Strawberries & cream

Avocado & lime

How much?

These recipes make enough for one face mask. Multiply the quantities by the number of guests you have.

Banana & honey

Put cucumber slices over your eyes for that super spa feeling.

Mash together!

- 2-3 strawberries
- 1 tbsp of heavy cream
- 1 tsp of honey

Honey makes your skin feel silky smooth.

Strawberries boost skin radiance.

Lime juice is good for balancing oily skin.

Avocados are great skin conditioners.

Mash together!

- ½ small avocado
- 1 tbsp of yogurt
- A squeeze of lime juice

Ripe bananas are rich moisturisers.

Mash together!

- 1 ripe banana
- 1 tsp of honey
- A squeeze of lemon juice

Lemon juice helps make your skin less shiny.

Hair flair

It's much more fun to create hairstyles with friends instead of on your own. Here are some ideas to get you started.

Twisted ponytail

1 Divide the hair into two sections. Twist one section tightly. Don't let go!

2 Now twist the other section in the same way.

3 Bring both sections together and twist them around each other. Secure with a hair elastic or ribbon.

Three-way braid

1 Divide the hair into three even sections. Braid each section and secure the ends.

A flower hides the hair elastics!

2 Braid the three sections together to make a larger braid.

Hair bow

1 Make a high ponytail and secure it with a hair elastic.

2 Pull the ponytail through the elastic until you have a loop.

3 Split the loop into two equal sections.

4 Bring the rest of the ponytail over the middle to finish the bow shape. Secure with *bobby pins*.

You can pin on a ribbon with a *bobby pin*.

Pretty maiden

1 Take three small, even sections from the front of the hair.

2 Braid together and secure with a hair elastic. Repeat on the other side of the head and secure the braids together at the back.

Add a pretty flower to complete the look.

21

Foot soak spa

Stuff you'll need!

- 10 tbsp of Epsom salts
- 2 tbsp baking soda
- 2 drops of essential oils
- Rose petals

Makes enough for 12!

Rose petals look lovely and can help soothe dry skin.

Running, dancing, jumping, we're always on our feet...

... so they deserve some TLC! Pamper your guests with your own DIY foot soak.

1 Measure the Epsom salts into a bowl, and then add the baking soda.

2 Add 2 drops of essential oils to make the foot soak smell delicious.

3 Stir it all together. Your homemade foot soak mixture is now ready.

Make sure the bowl is big enough for your feet.

4 To use, fill a bowl with warm water for each person and add 1 tbsp of the mixture to each bowl.

5 Top with rose petals. Soak your feet for 10 minutes, then rinse and dry. Bliss!

What type of friend are you?

Take this quiz to find out.

Are you the kind of friend who's always looking out for others, the jokey one who loves to laugh, or the one who organizes exciting activities?

Tell her right away—cringe!

Your friend has toilet paper stuck to her shoe. You...

It doesn't matter, so long as we spend time together.

Tell her, after a lot of giggling!

Start

What do you do on a day out with your friends?

Something fun, like going to the movies or going shopping.

Test what type of friend you are!

Your friend is feeling sad. You...

24

There's a new student at school and she seems a little shy. What do you do?

Say something friendly and show her around.

Caring & kind

You look after your friends and hate to see anyone sad. You and your close friends share everything.

Apologize and give her a hug.

Tell a funny story to put her at ease.

You can't go to your friend's birthday party! You...

Silly & fun

You know lots of jokes and love to make your friends laugh. They count on you to bring the fun, whatever the occasion.

Sit with her and have a cozy chat.

Try and arrange something to do when you're both free.

The joker—you love to giggle and have a good time.

Active & social

You love doing things with the people you like the most. You are always suggesting new activities and like to invite everyone along.

Take her out and try to make her laugh.

In a group of friends you are...

The organizer. You love getting everyone together.

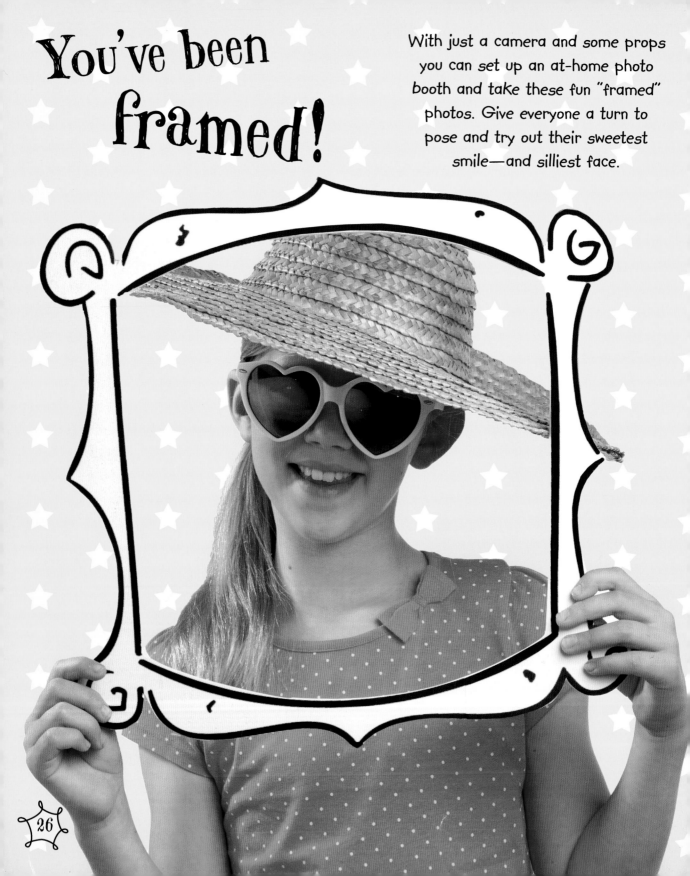

You've been framed!

With just a camera and some props you can set up an at-home photo booth and take these fun "framed" photos. Give everyone a turn to pose and try out their sweetest smile—and silliest face.

26

Stuff you'll need!

- Frame—use an old picture frame or draw a frame on cardboard, color it in, and cut it out.
- Funny hats, colorful sunglasses, feather boas, and any other accessories you can think of.
- A camera or a camera phone.

Giggly games

Not many parties can be planned with military precision, so there may be a moment or two when you're stuck for what to do next. But don't worry—we have some great game ideas!

Who am I?

Have everyone sit in a circle and secretly write the name of a famous person on a sticky note. Each person then sticks their note onto the forehead of the person sitting next to them (without letting that person see what's on the note). Everyone then takes turns asking questions with "yes" or "no" answers to figure out who they are.

The laughing game

Each person goes around in a circle and has to say either "Hee," "Ha," or "Ho." Anyone who starts laughing is out, until you have one (stony-faced) champion remaining!

Hairdo dash

Divide your guests into pairs, and get each pair to sit next to each other in a circle. Put lots of cheap hair accessories where everyone can reach them and set a five-minute time limit. The pairs have to grab what they can and style each other's hair before the time's up. Ask a grown-up to judge the winner.

Truth or dare

The classic sleepover party game! Each person has to choose whether to answer a "truth" question or do a "dare." Come up with a good question that the person must reveal the truth about, or something funny to do as a dare!

What's that song?

Play a song you think your guests will recognize. The first guest to correctly guess the song title gets one point, plus an extra point for naming the singer. Keep playing different songs until someone has 10 points.

Musical statues

Put on music and get everyone to dance. Pause the music at random points. Suddenly everyone must stand as still as a statue, in the position they were in when the music stopped. If you wobble, you're out! Keep playing until there's a winner.

Spin the nail polish bottle

Everyone sits in a circle holding a different nontoxic, peel-off polish. Take turns spinning a spare bottle in the middle (make sure the lid is screwed on tight!). The person the bottle points to has to paint one nail of each person with their color. Keep playing until you have a complete manicure. The person whose color was used most wins!

Guess the secret

Everyone has to write down something about herself that they think the others wouldn't know, and then put the notes (folded-up) in a bowl. One person at a time has to pull out a note and then read it aloud. Everyone has to try and guess whose secret it is!

29

Zodiac pals

Some people think your star sign may influence your personality. Find your sign on these pages—does the description match the type of friend you are?

Sagittarius
November 22—December 21

Perfect pals with: *Aries, Aquarius, Leo, Libra.* Sagittarians are bubbly, happy, and full of fun. They are very lively and always want to try new things.

Capricorn
December 22—January 19

Perfect pals with: *Pisces, Scorpio, Taurus, Virgo.* Capricorns are practical, sensible friends. They're wise, so they're good to go to for advice.

Garnet

Turquoise

Topaz

Scorpio
October 23—November 21

Perfect pals with: *Cancer, Capricorn, Pisces, Virgo.* It's hard to be bored with a Scorpio. They're fun and passionate and like to make sure that their friends are okay.

Opal

Sapphire

Peridot

Libra
September 23—October 22

Perfect pals with: *Aquarius, Gemini, Leo, Sagittarius.* If you're having trouble, ask a Libra for advice. Librans are calm, kind, and fair. They try to understand every point of view.

Virgo
August 23—September 22

Perfect pals with: *Cancer, Capricorn, Scorpio, Taurus.* Go to a Virgo when you need honest advice. They always want to help out their friends.

Leo
July 23—August 22

Perfect pals with: *Aries, Libra, Gemini, Sagittarius.* Leos are warm and bubbly. They're generally leaders of groups, just like the lion—their symbol.

Aquarius

January 20—February 18

Perfect pals with: Aries, Gemini, Libra, Sagittarius. Aquarians are imaginative and open-minded. They like coming up with quirky ideas.

Amethyst

Aquamarine

Diamond

Emerald

Pearl

Ruby

Pisces

February 19—March 20

Perfect pals with: Capricorn, Cancer, Scorpio, Taurus. Pisceans are kind, creative, and artistic—and may like to dance, paint, or sing!

Aries

March 21—April 19

Perfect pals with: Aquarius, Gemini, Leo, Sagittarius. Aries are the life and soul of a party. They're friendly and upbeat, but also like to be independent.

Taurus

April 20—May 20

Perfect pals with: Cancer, Capricorn, Pisces, Virgo. Taureans are down-to-earth and dependable. They're always up for doing fun things—especially if it involves fine food!

Birthstones

Each zodiac sign is represented by at least one birthstone. Look in the middle of the page to see what yours is—wearing it may bring you luck!

Gemini

May 21—June 20

Perfect pals with: Aries, Aquarius, Leo, Libra. Geminis are charming and lively. They find it easy to get along with different groups of people.

Cancer

June 21—July 22

Perfect pals with: Pisces, Scorpio, Taurus, Virgo. At first it might be hard to get to know a Cancer. But they're actually loving and caring friends.

Fortune-tellers

You don't need magical powers to predict the future—a fortune-teller does it for you! Try and invent hilarious fortunes that'll make you all giggle.

How many kids will I have—one, five, or 17!?

What will I be when I grow up—an actor, a pilot, a scientist, or a teacher?

Will I live in a castle, a mansion, a cottage, or a shack?

How to Play

Pick a color from the outside of the fortune-teller, for instance, "red"—three letters.

Open the fortune-teller once for each letter—sideways, up and down, sideways again.

Pick a number. Open the fortune-teller that many times.

Choose another number and open the flap to reveal your fortune!

Stuff you'll need!

- Square piece of paper
- Felt-tip pens

Fold the paper in half, top to bottom. Make a firm crease and unfold.

Fold again, this time from side to side, and unfold.

Fold a corner into the center and crease it down.

Do this again with each of the other corners.

Turn the square over. Fold a corner into the center.

Repeat with the other three corners, creasing each one firmly.

Fold the square in half, top to bottom. Make a crease and unfold.

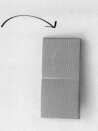

Fold again, side to side this time, then unfold.

Put your thumb and index fingers into the pockets and pick up the fortune-teller.

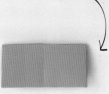

Draw different-colored pictures on the outside squares.

Write numbers on all the inside triangles.

It should look like this! Now fill in the outside squares and inside triangles.

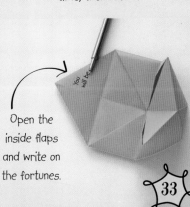

Open the inside flaps and write on the fortunes.

33

What type of fashionista are you?

Are you the sporty, wild, or glamorous type?

You have great taste and wear clothes that really suit you. But what fashion category do you fit into? Take this quiz to find out!

Going on a bike ride.

What sounds like more fun?

Wear something you feel happy and confident in.

Start
You're going to the school dance. You...

Going shopping.

Wear something quirky or glitzy— you love to sparkle!

Energetic and friendly.

Your friends would describe you as...

Trendy and hip.

I prefer to...

Be cool and comfortable.

You are an ultra-active fashionista. You mix pieces perfectly and look snazzy when relaxing or on the go.

Stand out from the crowd in jazzy designs.

Wild and Wonderful

Which of these would you choose to complete your outfit?

You are a colorful, quirky fashionista who is full of fun! Patterns and prints perfect your awesome look.

Glam and Girly

Which bag do you like best?

You are a super-swanky fashionista and aren't afraid to flaunt it. You look ultra hip and modern in the latest looks.

Flower power headbands

Ribbons add that finishing touch.

Put the flowers at a jaunty angle.

Use black and red tissue paper for poppies.

Headbands add fun and glamour to any outfit. These tissue paper delights are easy to make, and you and your friends can wear them as soon as you're done!

Stuff you'll need!

- Colored tissue paper
- Scissors
- Pipe cleaners
- Plain headband for each person
- Ribbon

1

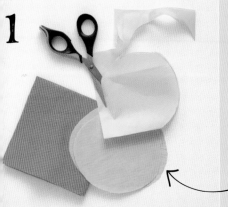

Fold the tissue paper so that it's about 10 layers thick. Cut a circle through all the layers. Do the same with all the tissue paper colors you want to use, making sure your circles are the same size.

3

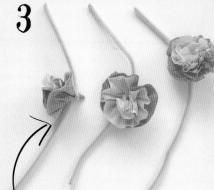

Firmly twist the pipe cleaner around the pinched base until it's secure. Then, starting from the middle, separate out each layer of tissue paper. Gently scrunch and crinkle the layers to create full and pretty petals.

Make a stack of your chosen circles (about 6-10 circles in total.) Hold the stack of circles in your hand and push into the center with your finger so that the sides curl up. Pinch the base tightly to create a flower shape.

2

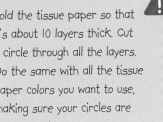
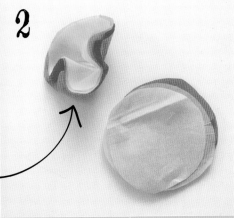

4

Attach the flowers by twisting the ends of the pipe cleaner around the headband. Cut off any excess.

Fold the ribbon in half and place it over the headband. Bring the ends through the loop to secure.

5

Enchanting eye masks

Can't sleep? A good way to get some shut-eye is to wear a comfy mask that blocks out the outside world. This fashionable one is fun to make with friends!

Stuff you'll need!

- Paper, pencil, and scissors
- Batting
- Colored felt
- Fabric pen, gems, and fabric glue
- Pins, embroidery needle, and thread
- Elastic (length to fit your head)

1

Trace the template on page 78 onto paper and cut it out. Place it on the batting and cut around the template with scissors.

You can trim the batting to make it a bit smaller than the felt.

Choose a color of felt that your fabric pen will show up on.

2

Use the paper template to cut out two pieces of felt for the front and back of the mask. Put the batting between the two pieces of felt, and pin all three layers together..

3

With an adult's help, thread your needle, Knot the end, and sew around the edges of the mask.

4

Sew the ends of the elastic to the back of the mask. It's now ready to decorate! Use the fabric pen (keep it away from your clothes and any furniture), then glue on the gems using fabric glue.

Embellish the mask with pretty gems.

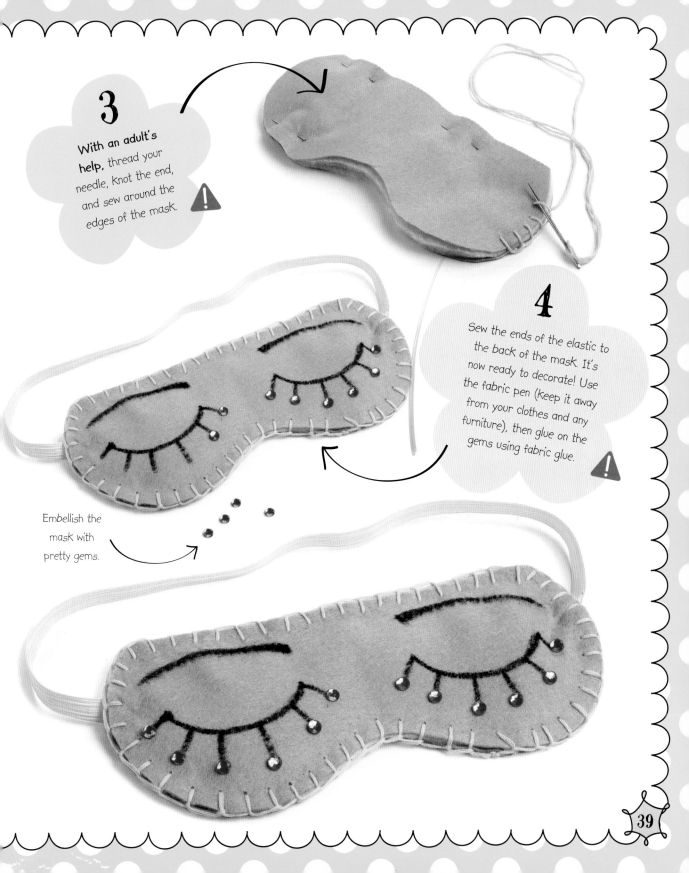

Felt fun

These felty wonders are great for just about anything—tie them to your bag, hang them up as decorations, or pin them to your jacket. The possibilities are endless, so let your imagination run wild!

1

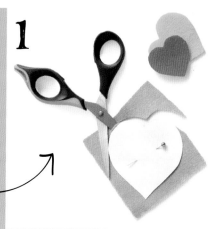

⚠️ Trace the templates on page 78 onto paper (you can choose hearts or flowers). Cut out the templates and pin each one to a different-colored piece of felt. Then carefully cut around each template.

Stuff you'll need!

- Paper
- Felt squares in different colors
- Pins and scissors
- Buttons in different colors
- Needle and thread
- Ribbons

2

Make a pile of your shapes with the smallest ones on top. Choose two or three buttons and stack them on the front. **With the help of an adult**, thread your needle and knot the end of your thread.

3

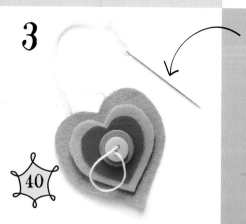

40

Holding it all together, start at the back and pass the needle and thread through all the layers and one set of buttonholes, then go back through the other buttonholes. Do this a few times, then make a knot at the back. ⚠️

Sew a ribbon to the back to hang up your decoration.

4

Dreamcatchers

Native Americans make dreamcatchers to catch bad dreams. They are perfect for sleepovers. Make one together and hang it in your bedroom.

Stuff you'll need!

- Embroidery hoop or hoop made from craft wire
- Ribbon
- Glue
- Embroidery thread or string
- Beads and feathers for decoration

You can use craft wire to make a hoop.

1

Start by wrapping the hoop with the ribbon. Secure with a little glue at both ends.

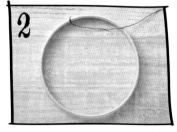

2

Knot one end of the thread tightly around the hoop.

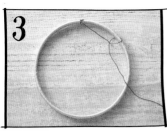

3

Loop the thread around the hoop as shown. Pull the thread to tighten it.

4

Continue around the hoop, making evenly spaced loops until you get back to the start knot.

5

Start a second round, this time making loops around the centers of the sections.

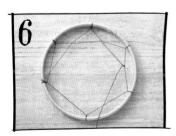

6

Continue until you finish the second round. Try to keep the thread tight.

7

Keep making rounds in this way and thread on beads as you work toward the middle.

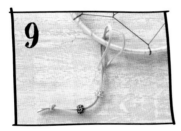

8

When you reach the middle, secure with a knot. Cut off the extra thread.

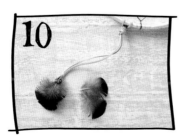

9

Take a length of string, double it over, and thread on beads. Knot the end. Loop over the hoop to attach.

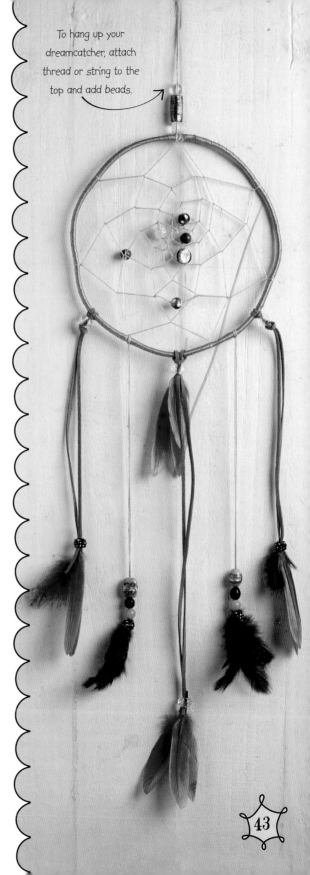

10

Repeat step 9 four more times. Push feathers into the bead holes—pack tightly so they won't fall out.

To hang up your dreamcatcher, attach thread or string to the top and add beads.

What's your ideal costume?

What are you destined to become next?

If you can't decide on a costume, try this quick quiz. You'll find out what will suit your personality best.

Start

You are somewhere new with lots of people you have never met before. What do you do first?

Go and chat to people.

Be able to fly.

Speak to animals.

Which of these magical powers would you most like to have? To...

You are more suited for a life in...

What sounds like more fun?

An enchanted forest.

The wide-open prairies.

Horseback riding.

Colorful Fairy

You are sugary sweet and super friendly. Put on a pair of wings, get your wand ready, and ta-da—a magical transformation right before your eyes!

Wild West Hero

Yee-haw! Go lasso your hat, bandanna, and checkered shirt, and let's head on down to the rodeo, Partner!

Watch and observe.

You prefer...

Nighttime.

Daytime.

Garlic—do you love it or hate it?

It's alright— never done me any harm...

Urgh, get it away from me!

Can you be quite secretive?

Your ideal afternoon would be...

Not often.

Sometimes.

Gymnastics.

Going out on on adventure.

At home with friends.

No-nonsense Ninja

Go grab your black clothes and a fake sword—you are clearly an undercover superhero! You will look so cool sneaking around.

Glam Vampire

False teeth, white face paint, and a cape are all you need to look scarily fabulous. Just don't go out in sunlight!

Chunky bangles

Jangly bracelets add a pretty decoration to your wrist and show off your funky fashion sense. Make your own supereasy bead bangles.

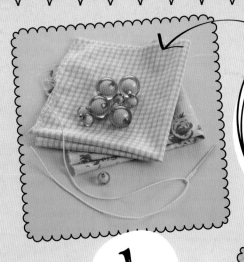

Stuff you'll need!
- Cotton fabric and scissors
- Beads—large and small
- Elastic thread
- Darning needle (if you want)

1

Make a small snip into the fabric with the scissors, then pull off a strip with your hands so the sides are ragged. Make around 6 strips for each bracelet.

2

Thread beads onto the elastic, alternating large and small ones. You can do this with your hands, or **ask an adult** to help you thread them with a darning needle.

Mix different cotton fabrics for a funky effect.

3

When the bracelet is long enough to fit comfortably around your wrist, tie the ends in a knot. Then tie the cloth strips over the elastic between the beads.

Lucky charms

These sweet charms look good enough to eat! You can make them into key rings or matching necklaces for everyone.

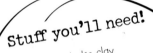

Stuff you'll need!

- Oven-bake clay
- Wooden modeling tool
- Beads for decoration
- Small screw eyes
- Ribbons or key rings

Make a tiny doughnut by sticking a thin disk on a thick one. Then make the hole with your modeling tool.

1

For a tiny cupcake, shape the clay into three ¾in (2cm) balls for the cupcake, case, and frosting. Make a smaller ball to go on top.

2

Shape the case so it's smaller at the top and larger on the bottom. Flatten each end. Use a modeling tool to make side folds as shown.

3

Flatten the top and bottom of the cupcake, making sure it's wider than your case. Press the case onto your cupcake.

4

Roll the frosting into a long sausage, making it smaller toward one end. Then, starting at the narrow end, shape it into a swirl!

For a hamburger, make three thick disks for the meat and buns. Don't forget the cheese and lettuce!

You can use real sprinkles to decorate your sweet creations!

5

Turn your cupcake and case the right way up. Firmly attach the frosting to the top of the cake.

6

Press beads into the frosting for decoration. Then add the small ball of clay on the top so it looks like a cherry.

7

Press the screw eye into the top. **Ask an adult** to bake your charm in the oven according to the clay manufacturer's instructions.

8

Make sure your charm has cooled down. Then attach a pretty ribbon or a key ring to the screw eye.

Rings and things

Stuff you'll need!
- Assorted beads
- Craft wire
- Pliers to help you hold and twist the wire.
- Scissors

Twisted bead ring

Bead band rings

Try out lots of color combinations!

50

Making these bling rings is an awesome party activity that lets everyone get creative, colorful, and crafty. Even better—guests can take them home afterward!

How to make a twisted bead ring

1

Thread a big bead onto a 5in (12cm) length of wire. Twist the wire around the bead to hold it in place.

2

Thread smaller beads onto the wire until you're about ¾in (2cm) from the end.

3

Add another big bead to the end, then wind the wire around the bead.

4

Snip off any excess wire. Wrap the ring around your finger to get the right fit.

How to make a bead band ring

1

Thread one large bead onto a 10in (25cm) length of wire. Add a small bead on each side.

2

Center the beads on the wire, then put another large bead on one side.

3

Feed the other end of the wire back through the same bead, in the other direction.

4

Pull both ends of the wire to close the gap, then add two more small beads.

5

Keep repeating steps 2–4 until the ring fits around your finger.

6

To finish off, bring the end of the wire back through the bead you started with.

7

Feed the other end of the wire through this bead, too, but in the opposite direction.

8

Tighten, then twist the wire around the bead to secure. Snip off the extra wire.

Stuff you'll need!

- Ribbon (enough to wrap around your wrist and a little extra for the bow)
- Candies with holes or soft candy
- Scissors
- Needle and thread (for soft candy without holes)

With an adult's help, you can use a needle and thread to make a bracelet from soft candies that don't have holes.

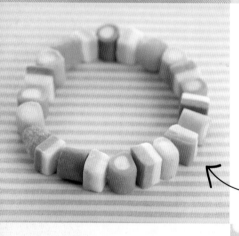

Candy bangles

These supersweet bracelets couldn't be easier to make. Just thread a ribbon through the center of your candies, tie it on your wrist, make a bow—and ta-da! (Try not to eat the bracelet right away.)

What's your inner animal?

What's the animal inside YOU?

Are you a friendly dolphin, a cool cat, or a wise owl? Take this quiz to find out which cute critter you secretly are....

2

Do you like swimming?

A: You love it—you're basically a fish!
B: You'll paddle—and keep your hair dry!
C: No! You'd rather sit by the water and watch the world go by.

1

You're going to the movies. What type of movie do you choose?

A: A comedy—you love a good laugh.
B: An old black-and-white movie—you're very sophisticated, you see.
C: A historical drama where all the characters are dressed up.

Mostly A's: Dolphin

You're a cheerful, energetic dolphin. You make everything fun and you love to laugh. Even the grumpiest person can't be angry when you're around!

Most B's: Cat

You're an independent, cool cat. You know what suits you and you stick with it. Your special friends love you because you're so charming.

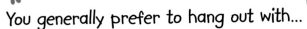

3

You generally prefer to hang out with...
A: A large group of friends.
B: One friend who is important to you.
C: A few close friends.

4

Someone asks you to clean your room. What do you do?
A: You only do a bit of cleaning up—you'd rather go out and play.
B: You don't do it—what a ridiculous question!
C: You do it quickly, but then take a nice nap.

5

What would you rather do for fun with friends?
A: Go outside and play games.
B: Do something a little different, such as rock climbing or painting.
C: Play board games at home.

Mostly C's: Owl

You're a clever and wise owl. You're a great listener with smart and sensible ideas. People turn to you when they need advice because you're always calm and have something helpful to say.

No-sew tutus

Hey, there, young stars-to-be! You should totally dance and prance around the house wearing these funky tutus. They're just great for dressing up and putting on a show!

Stuff you'll need!

- 6½ft (2 meters) tulle fabric
- Ribbon
- Scissors

1 Cut a long length of ribbon for the waistband. Cut the tulle into strips that are 5in (12cm) wide and at least 3ft (1 meter) long. Fold each strip in half, place it over the ribbon, and bring the ends through the loop to secure.

2

Keep adding strips of tulle to the ribbon. Shuffle them together to make the tutu full and fluffy. For that extra something, you can add lengths of ribbon—or even different colored tulle—at various points as you go along.

3

When you've knotted enough material around the ribbon waistband, tie the two ends together around your waist. Make a pretty bow and snip off any excess.

Transform your sneakers

Fed up with plain, dull footwear? Here's a fun way to get creative and add a colorful kick to some boring, bland shoes!

Stuff you'll need!

- Pair of clean canvas sneakers
- Pencil and eraser
- Black and colored fabric markers
- Ribbon (if you like)

1

Remove the laces from your canvas sneakers. Your first job is to draw your design. Use a pencil so you can erase any mistakes. You can also plan your design on paper before you start.

You can erase mistakes at this stage.

2

Get out your black fabric marker and draw over the outlines of your design. **Always be careful with your markers. Keep them away from your clothes and the furniture because they can stain.**

3

Once you have drawn your outline design, it's time to get colorful! Using your colored markers, carefully color in your sneakers. You can be as creative as you want. Go color mad or just use a couple of colors—it's up to you.

4

As a finishing touch, add some colorful ribbon for new laces. You can also use yarn or cord.

Hair wraps

Hair wraps look cool and are so simple to make. Our clever wraps clip in and out, so you can try lots of styles!

Stuff you'll need!

- Embroidery thread
- Safety pin
- Beads
- Hair clips

Starting off

Take several lengths of thread about 3ft (1m) long. Loop them through a safety pin so that they are doubled over.

Tie a knot at the top of your threads. You're now ready to start making bands of color and spirals in any order you like!

⚠️ Attach the safety pin to a pillow to keep the wraps steady and your hands free.

One-color band

Take a couple of the threads that are one color and wrap them tightly around the other threads.

Keep wrapping until your first band is 1in (3cm) long. Secure it by pulling the threads through the last wrap.

Single spiral

To make a spiral, pull out one or two threads. Wrap around with another color to make a 1in (3cm) band.

Take the threads you left at the top and spiral them down over the top of the band.

Double spiral

To make a double spiral, make a single spiral, but pull out an extra thread and leave it behind.

Take the extra thread and spiral down the band in the opposite direction. Cool!

To finish

When the wrap is long enough, thread a bead (or two) onto the end. Make a knot, then trim the excess threads.

Remove the safety pin and replace with a cool hair clip. Ta-da! It's ready to clip on and wear.

61

Funky flip-flops

Here's a way of jazzing up your favorite flip-flops. You'll love showing off your style in the sun or on the beach.

Stuff you'll need!

- Flip-flops
- Cotton fabric, pom-poms, or ribbon
- Strong glue
- Scissors

1

Rip your fabric into ½in (1cm) wide strips. Make a small snip, then pull the strip off with your hands for a ragged effect.

Match the fabric to your flip-flops or use a clashing color for a bold look.

2

Loop each strip over the flip-flop strap and pull the ends through the loop to secure it in place.

3

Keep adding strips until the straps are completely covered. And, you're ready! Time to step out and show the world!

Aren't these just so funky?

Pom-poms

Fuzzy pom-poms add a nice touch. Stick them on with strong glue and then let them dry.

You can alternate colors or use one color for a simpler look.

Squishy pom-poms look wild and feel comfy.

Ribbons

Tying on equal lengths of ribbon gives a clean and stylish look.

What are you destined to do?

Let's gaze into the crystal ball to see your future...

Take this quiz to find out if you're going to be an adventurous scientist, an awesome boss, or a super-savvy stylist.

1

Where would you most like to go on vacation?
A: To a big city.
B: On safari.
C: To a beach.

2

Your ideal birthday present would be...
A: Money to save for a rainy day.
B: Lots of really interesting books.
C: Tickets to your favorite concert—with an amazing outfit to wear.

Mostly A's: High-Flying Boss

You're such a good leader; you're destined to be an awesome boss. The big city is calling your name. You will be very rich and live at the top of a skyscraper with spectacular views.

3 What sport would you like to be good at?
A: A team sport—although you would have to be the captain.
B: Car racing—it's fun, fast, and technical.
C: Ice-skating—the sparklier the outfit, the better!

4

Two of your friends are arguing. What do you do?
A: Talk to them together and help them make up.
B: Talk to each of them alone and try to understand both sides.
C: Tell a joke to make them laugh. Life's too short for arguments!

5

You find a monster hidden in your room. It's very scared. What do you do?
A: Have a chat and arrange for it to be reunited with its family.
B: Examine it and ask questions about where it came from.
C: Make friends and invite it to your next party.

Mostly B's: Scientist

You'll be an adventurous scientist. You could work in a submarine or trek through the rain forest. You might even make amazing discoveries in a top-secret laboratory!

Mostly C's: Super Stylist

You're clearly going to be a number-one fashion stylist. You will live in a big mansion by the beach, attend glitzy parties, and everyone will want to wear your creations.

Mocktails

Ooh, la, la! Could there *be* anything more sophisticated than sipping on stylish mocktails? Here are some awesome ideas—all you need to do is mix up the ingredients.

Fancy straws are fun and look great, too.

Find the templates for these pretty straw decorations on page 79.

Shirley Temple
- 1 glass ginger ale
- 1 tbsp grenadine syrup
- Ice

Mock Mojito
- 1 glass lemonade
- Crushed mint leaves
- Squeeze of lime
- Ice, and cucumber slice to garnish

Cheat's Champagne
- ½ glass ginger ale
- ½ glass apple juice

Tropical Cooler
- ½ glass pineapple juice
- ½ glass orange juice
- Cocktail cherries and lemon slice to garnish

Dip glass rims in orange juice, then into sugar or crushed candies.

Prepare your mocktails in pitchers for a bigger group.

Cranberry Delight

- 1/2 glass apple juice
- 1/2 glass cranberry juice
- Strawberry to garnish

Pink Fizz

- 1 pitcher sparkling elderflower
- Squeeze of lime
- Splash of cranberry juice for color

St. Clement's

- 1/2 pitcher orange juice
- 1/2 pitcher lemonade
- Orange and lime slices to garnish

Perfect popcorn

Popcorn is the perfect party snack, and it's really easy to make. Add cheese or chocolate for an extra tasty treat that everyone will love.

Stuff you'll need!
- 1 tbsp sunflower oil
- ½ cup popcorn kernels
- 1oz (40g) cheese (and turmeric, if you want)
- 1½oz (25g) chocolate

1 Get an adult to heat the oil in a saucepan. Stir in the popcorn and cover. Wait for the popping to begin!

2 When the popping slows, shake the pan. Remove when you hear just a few pops per second.

Ask an adult to melt the chocolate in a heatproof bowl over boiling water.

You can add a pinch of turmeric for color and flavor.

Chocolate
Spread the popcorn on a baking sheet. Get an adult to melt the chocolate, then drizzle it over the popcorn. Let cool.

Cheese
Grate the cheese over the popcorn while it's warm. Ask an adult to put it under a hot broiler for 30 seconds to melt the cheese.

68

The recipe makes one large bowl of popcorn.

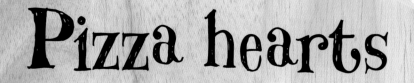

Pizza hearts

These hearty pizzas are as delightful as they are delicious. For a treat everyone will love, let your guests choose their own toppings.

Stuff you'll need!

- 4 cups flour, plus extra to dust
- A pinch of salt
- 4 tsp olive oil
- 2½ tsp active dry yeast
- 1½ cups warm water
- Tomato paste
- Cheese
- A selection of toppings

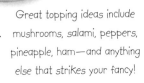

Great topping ideas include mushrooms, salami, peppers, pineapple, ham—and anything else that strikes your fancy!

1

Mix the flour, salt, and oil in a large bowl. In a small bowl, mix the yeast and warm water. Leave for five minutes. Slowly stir the yeast mixture into the flour mixture with a wooden spoon.

2

Put flour on your hands and work surface. Knead the dough for 10 minutes, flattening it and folding it in half with your palm.

Ask an adult to help you knead the dough.

3

Put the dough back in the bowl and cover with plastic wrap or a dish towel. Let rest for about an hour—until it's doubled in size. After that, push your fist into the dough to knock out excess air and knead one more time.

Dough needs to rest in a warm place so it will rise.

4

Roll the dough onto a floured surface and cut out heart shapes. Add the tomato paste, toppings, and cheese. **Ask an adult** to cook the pizzas in a 425°F (220°C) oven for 10 minutes, or until golden.

Ice cream parlor

Ice cream is—quite literally—the coolest of all party snacks. Gather lots of tasty toppers and whip up your own sundae bar. Your friends will be so impressed!

Lay out bowls and spoons for everyone, and, of course, lots of ice cream cones.

Fill bowls with different candies, sprinkles, cookies, and tasty fruit.

Everyone can make a special dream sundae!

Don't forget yummy sauces, whipped cream, and cherries for the top!

73

Good-bye goodies

It's always nice to give a little something to your guests to thank them for coming to your party. Here are some ideas that will finish off your sleepover on the best possible note!

Sweet Treats

Retro-style candy jars make great vintage gifts. Fill them with lots of tasty, colorful delights!

Sundae Best

Create a pamper-time sundae in a plastic sundae glass. First, add bath salts, then a bath pouf, and top with a small bath bead. To finish, add an emery board and tie on a gift tag.

Funky Frames

Make a cardboard photo frame and decorate with gemstones or stickers for each of your guests. Guests can put a favorite picture from the party inside it!.

Fashion Swag Bag

For a fashion-themed party bag, give hair clips, nail polish, jewelry, and other fun, fashion stuff!

Tie a ribbon around for that final flourish.

Pamper Present

Do something different and give your gift at the *beginning* of a pamper party. Wrap a ribbon around a toothbrush and washcloth so it seems like your guests have arrived at a swanky hotel!

Camping Rations

Fill a bag with camping-themed goodies, such as marshmallows, gummy worms, and a mini flashlight. For a personal touch, make a friendship bracelet for each guest and add it to the bag.

Rock Star Kit

Create a playlist with your favorite tunes so guests can rock out for the following few weeks.

Showtime Supplies

Print off an awards certificate for each guest who attends your party. Put it in a movie-themed party pack, filled with superstar stickers, a small bag of candies—and lots of popcorn, of course!

Bath Salt Delight

Get a pretty jar and fill it with bath salts. Or why not add in the foot spa mix from page 22?

Write your guests' names on the labels.

Sarah

Kayleigh

Templates

Copy these templates to help make the projects in the book.

How to use: All you have to do is use a pencil to trace the templates onto thin paper. Turn the paper over, then draw over your pencil lines to transfer the pictures onto stiff paper or card stock. Cut out each shape and you'll have a template to draw around.

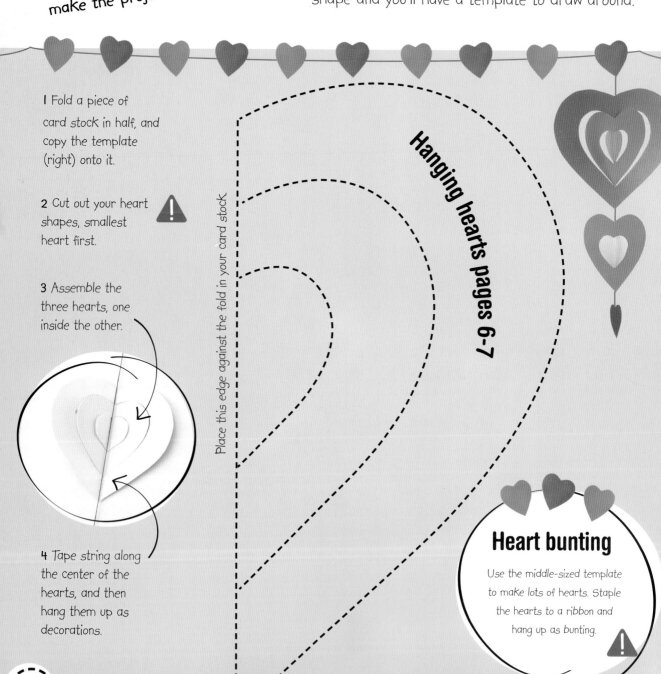

1 Fold a piece of card stock in half, and copy the template (right) onto it.

2 Cut out your heart shapes, smallest heart first.

3 Assemble the three hearts, one inside the other.

4 Tape string along the center of the hearts, and then hang them up as decorations.

Place this edge against the fold in your card stock

Hanging hearts pages 6-7

Heart bunting

Use the middle-sized template to make lots of hearts. Staple the hearts to a ribbon and hang up as bunting.

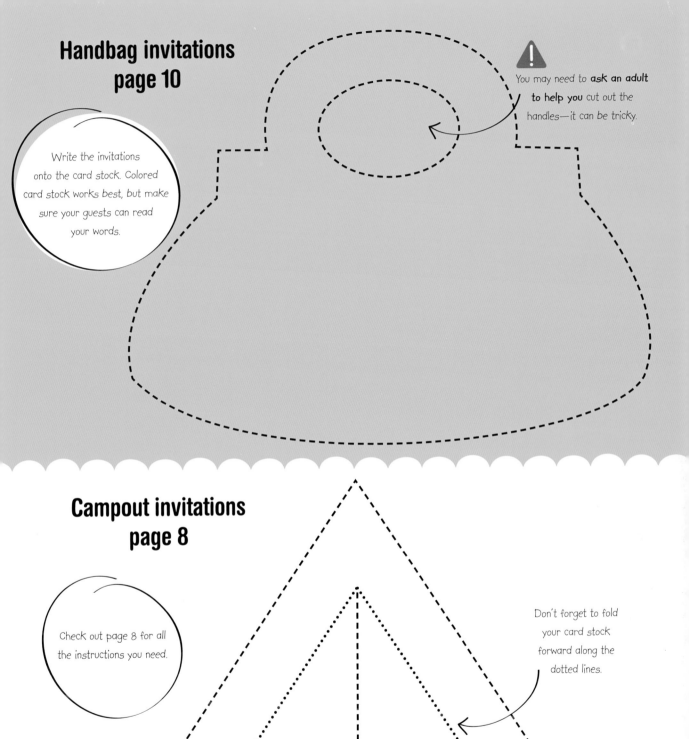

Handbag invitations
page 10

Write the invitations onto the card stock. Colored card stock works best, but make sure your guests can read your words.

You may need to **ask an adult to help you** cut out the handles—it can be tricky.

Campout invitations
page 8

Check out page 8 for all the instructions you need.

Don't forget to fold your card stock forward along the dotted lines.

Eye mask
pages 38-39

If you are making eye masks with your guests, you can be super organized and make your templates before the party starts.

You can also use this template for your invitations on page 7.

Felt fun
pages 40-41

Mocktail straw decorations
pages 66-67

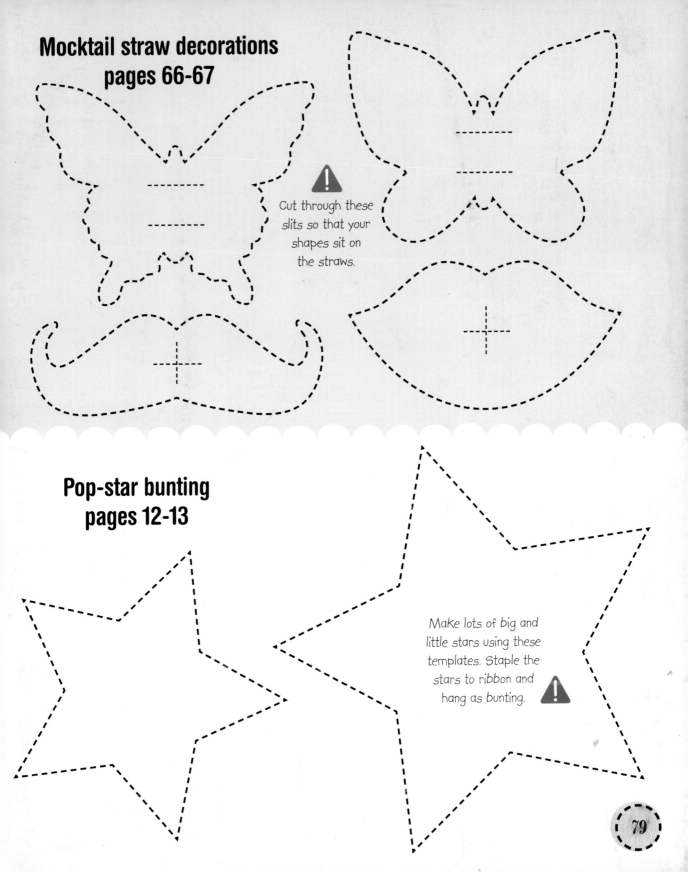

Cut through these slits so that your shapes sit on the straws.

Pop-star bunting
pages 12-13

Make lots of big and little stars using these templates. Staple the stars to ribbon and hang as bunting.

79

Index

DK would like to thank

Dawn Sirett and Carrie Love for proofreading, Rosie Levine for jacket assistance, Kate Blinman for help with the recipes, and Charlotte Milner for illustrations.

With special thanks to the models: Lottie Burridge, Sahara Dosku, Lizzie Greenstreet, Jemimah Haque, Annabel Meadows, Ella Russell, Fatima Soltani, Sophie Tovell, Lucy Williams, Lilyann Yven-Dent, and Sophia Zaghetta.

31901059420788